Overcoming

Challenges

The Life of Charles F. Bolden, Jr.

Written by Darwin McBeth Walton

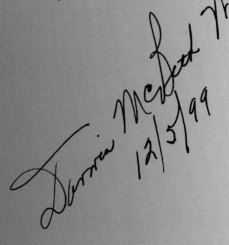

Darwin McBeth Walton
12/5/99

STECK-VAUGHN
COMPANY

A Division of Harcourt Brace & Company

www.steck-vaughn.com

Contents

Major events in the life of Charles F. Bolden, Jr.

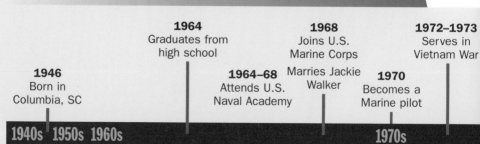

1946
Born in
Columbia, SC

1964
Graduates from
high school

1964–68
Attends U.S.
Naval Academy

1968
Joins U.S.
Marine Corps

Marries Jackie
Walker

1970
Becomes a
Marine pilot

1972–1973
Serves in
Vietnam War

1940s 1950s 1960s   1970s

Chapter 1
The First Countdown

Do you ever wonder what it feels like to travel through space? Are you curious about what it's like to be an astronaut? Maybe you've even thought of becoming one!

Astronauts do scientific experiments. They put satellites into orbit. They take pictures of stars and galaxies. Like Charles F. Bolden, Jr., they pilot space shuttles, too.

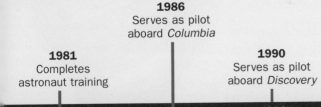

1981
Completes astronaut training

1986
Serves as pilot aboard *Columbia*

1990
Serves as pilot aboard *Discovery*

1998
Becomes Deputy Commander of U.S. forces in Japan

Becomes a major general in U.S. Marines

1980s   1990s   2000s

Imagine floating like a balloon as you work. Think about seeing Earth from 200 miles (322 kilometers) away! Imagine listening to the countdown for the **launch** of your space shuttle. On December 18, 1985, Pilot Charles F. Bolden, Jr., was ready to do all that.

Dressed in his space suit and strapped in his seat on the space shuttle *Columbia*, Charles listened to **Mission Control**. When he was young, no one would have guessed he would someday sit in a spaceship. But in spite of the **obstacles** he had faced, he was there. His heart pounded. No doubt about it, this was the most awesome thing he had done in his whole life!

The other crew members were strapped in their seats, too. Commander Robert "Hoot" Gibson headed the mission. Steven Hawley, George "Pinkey" Nelson, and Dr. Franklin Chang-Diaz

Columbia crew members wore this special patch on their uniforms.

served as the other crew members. Robert Cenker and Florida congressman Bill Nelson sat aboard to look on.

All the crew members had studied different sciences for years. They had trained together for months. They had learned every detail about flying the *Columbia*, including how to work in zero **gravity**, where everything floats.

The *Columbia* crew heads for the space shuttle on December 18, 1995.

As Charles sat in his pilot's seat, he felt physically fit and ready for the **challenge** of space. But with only 15 minutes left in the countdown, the computer called for the engines to shut down. Something was wrong. The computer had found a broken part.

Charles and Commander Gibson were trained to react quickly to computer warnings. They knew about the dangerous things that could happen on a shuttle launch. They quickly turned off the launch controls. Everyone left the space shuttle.

From left to right, George Nelson, Steven Hawley, Robert Gibson, Franklin Chang-Diaz, and Charles F. Bolden, Jr.

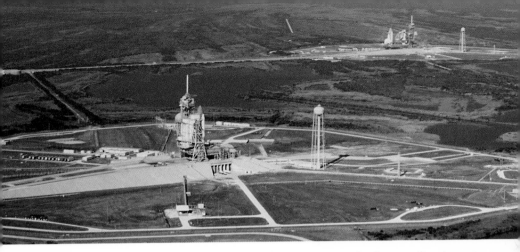

Kennedy Space Center at Cape Canaveral, Florida

The crew knew that the breakdown meant another delay. They were disappointed.

Charles's mother, Ethel Bolden, was also disappointed. She had traveled all the way from South Carolina to the Kennedy Space Center in Florida to see the launch. She later said, "The delay was nerve-wracking for me."

Charles's wife, Jackie, had mixed feelings. She knew how much this voyage meant to Charles. But she worried about his safety.

During the delay, Charles went home to Houston, Texas, to wait for the shuttle to be fixed. Then Florida was hit by rain and storms. The delay lasted for weeks. It was **frustrating** to wait, but the crew knew that they had no choice.

Charles's children, Anthony Ché and Kelly, were glad to be with their dad for Christmas in Houston. Still, Ché and Kelly were excited about their dad's first space voyage. They wanted their father to fly into space. Most of their friends were also interested in the space program.

Ché and Kelly and their friends knew that the mission would put a satellite into orbit. The satellite would send TV and radio signals from one part of the world to another. The crew members would also take photographs of Halley's Comet. They would carry out experiments such as studying crystals, too

The satellite that *Columbia* put into orbit

Chapter 2

Liftoff!

At last, on January 12, 1986, the rain stopped. The crew boarded *Columbia* again. Through the shuttle's cabin window, Charles could see a few stars twinkling in the early morning sky. He tried to ignore the nervous feeling in his stomach. He thought about his family waiting 3 miles away on the roof of the launch control center.

Charles's one wish was that his dad had lived to see this dream come true. "I'm doing it, Dad," he whispered to himself. "But I believe Mom's scared to death."

His thoughts of his parents stopped when he heard Mission Control. "We're 5 minutes away from countdown. We're ready for a 6:55 A.M. liftoff," a voice said.

Charles paid close attention to the controls.

"Charlie, you okay?" Franklin Chang-Diaz's voice came through Charles's helmet.

"Yeah, sure, I'm great. How about you? Are you ready to fly?"

"You know how long I've been looking forward to this?" asked Franklin. "Think of all the people who would like to be in our place."

"Quite a few, I'll bet," Charles answered. "Got your camera ready? Try to take some pictures when we start floating. My children don't believe

that in zero gravity even gum wrappers and dirt will float. A photo might help convince Ché."

Then Mission Control said, "We are just a little more than 2 minutes away from countdown. The computer will now take over the launch and will monitor the shuttle systems."

"Charlie, ready to go for launch?" asked Commander Gibson.

"Roger. Let's go for launch!" Charles replied. He tried to stay cool.

Commander Gibson spoke to Mission Control. "This is *Columbia*. Everything looks good."

Charles could hardly control his excitement. This was the moment he had dreamed of his whole life.

"*T* minus 30 seconds and counting." Mission Control was giving the final orders and checking all of the systems.

Charles heard the countdown clearly. He shivered in spite of himself. Then he heard Mission Control say, "We have main engine start! Four, three, two, one! Ignition and liftoff!"

◀ **In training, the astronauts learned how to move around in zero gravity.**

From his seat Charles watched the fiery glow of the rockets. Then 3 billion gallons (11 billion liters) of water were released. A huge white cloud of steam shot from the launch pad as the shuttle lifted off into the dark sky. The thrust of the rockets pressed the men into their seats. The shuttle shook so much that Charles could barely read the cockpit **gauges**.

The *Columbia* liftoff

Chapter 3

Another Alarm

Suddenly an alarm went off. Something else had gone wrong! All eyes turned to Charles as he scanned the instrument panel for the problem. He quickly located a message on the monitor and turned to Commander Gibson. "Looks like we might have a helium leak on the right engine!" Charles told the commander. "I'm closing the *A* **regulator** on that side!"

Commander Gibson studied the monitor and then spoke to Mission Control. "This is *Columbia*. Charlie just located a bad regulator on the right engine."

The official *Columbia* photograph

Mission Control told the crew to hold on. The crew waited as the shuttle flew on. A few minutes later, Mission Control told *Columbia* to increase the engine power.

"Roger, Houston. Let's go!" said Commander Gibson. Then he turned to Charles. "Charlie, how are things looking?"

"Everything looks okay now," answered Charles. He breathed a loud sigh of relief. "But that was some shake, rattle, and roll."

"Yeah, Charlie, your eyes are still crossed," Steven Hawley said with a chuckle.

"This is Mission Control. Two minutes into flight, and main engines look great!"

Gibson, Bolden, and Hawley continued to watch the closed regulator. Gibson said, "Charlie, let's reopen that regulator. I think it's still good."

Charles opened the regulator. He studied the computer.

Charles at work on the *Columbia*.

15

For the next few minutes, the crew talked about what to do. Commander Gibson explained that it was still possible to stop the mission.

The shuttle could return to Kennedy Space Center. Or the crew could decide to fly over the Atlantic Ocean and watch the regulator to see what would happen. "What do you say, Charlie?" asked Commander Gibson.

"The engine looks good," replied Charles. "Let's keep going."

"Roger," said Commander Gibson. He told Mission Control that *Columbia* would continue on its mission.

Charles's eyes were on the clock. "No turning back now. We'll be outside Earth's gravity in seconds," he told the rest of the crew.

As the main engine shut off, the cabin became totally quiet. After a while Charles felt his body fluids shift upward, as if he were coming out of his skin. Without any help from him, his arms floated up to eye level. He was in zero gravity. He was weightless, like a giant puppet. The feeling was like nothing he had ever felt on Earth!

After shouts of joy, the crew waited to get used to being without gravity. It took a while for them to get used to being weightless. They unbuckled their harnesses. One by one they came out of their seat belts. They flew and tumbled around the cabin. "The guys acted like ten-year-olds," Charles later remembered.

Every item on board was tacked down. Even books and pencils were attached to tabletops with special fasteners.

The *Columbia* crew has fun being weightless.

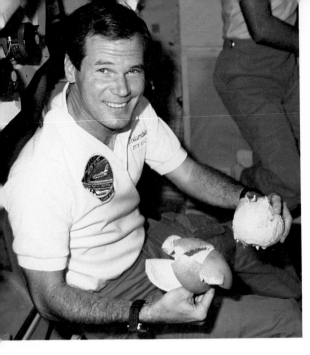

Congressman Bill Nelson gets ready to eat a grapefruit in space.

"Eating was a real trick," Charles recalled. "Except for things like bread and candy, we squeezed all our food from plastic tubes directly into our mouths. We had containers with capped straws. Otherwise, the liquid would float right out of the cup. We added water or liquid to dried foods, like onion and spinach soup, to make them edible. It tasted good if we didn't have to look at it."

The men slept on air. "That was fun," Charles said later, "and comfortable, too." To keep from floating into someone else's space, they hooked an arm or a leg through a strap. To sleep in bright light, they put on sleep masks.

Columbia's six-day flight went off with only minor problems. The communications satellite was placed in orbit, and the experiments went as scheduled. Still, getting off the ground had been a problem. The crew had endured breakdowns and many delays.

"However, it was the thrill of a lifetime," said Charles after they made a safe return landing. "I for one am ready to go again!"

The shuttle has a special kind of parachute to help it slow down.

Chapter 4

Little Charles

Charles's father, Charles, Sr., was a coach and gym teacher at Carver School in Columbia, South Carolina. When Charles, Sr., went into the U.S. Army in 1943, he and his sweetheart, Ethel Martin, decided to marry right away. But they had to keep their marriage a secret because Ethel was a teacher, too. At that time, schoolteachers (especially women) in South Carolina were not allowed to marry.

Charles, Sr., served in Africa and was on his way to Okinawa, Japan, when the war ended on August 14, 1945. He returned to his bride and to his job at Carver School.

One year later, on August 19, 1946, Charles, Jr., was born. Because he was named after his dad, Ethel called him "Little Charles." The name stuck all through his early years, probably because he was smaller than other children his age.

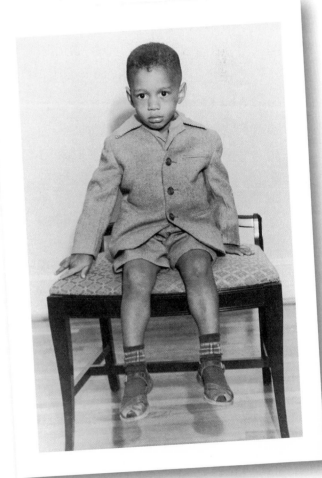

Charles, Jr., at age 4

Being the smallest kid on the block was not much fun. Little Charles had to deal with problems that larger children don't know about. Once, in first grade, two bigger boys stopped him on the way to school and took his milk money. Charles didn't tell his mother or his teacher, but he worried about it all day. He thought about it that night before he went to sleep.

The next morning Charles put a dime in each one of his shoes and a nickel in his pocket. The bigger boys took the nickel, but they missed the two dimes. For the next few days, Charles didn't have a nickel in his pocket. But he had milk at lunch because he had left the two dimes safely hidden in his desk.

During elementary school, Charles was often left out of games and sports because of his size. Most of the other boys were taller than he was. Even his younger brother, Warren, was taller than Charles by the time Charles was 12.

Warren's size was a problem for Charles. Warren thought that because he was bigger than his older brother, he should be allowed to stay around Charles and Charles's friends. Charles complained to his mom and dad. He sometimes gave Warren marbles or candy so that Warren would leave him alone. For a while nothing seemed to work. Finally Warren lost interest and found friends his own age.

Little Charles (on the left) and his brother, Warren, in 1954

Charles learned to swim in elementary school. Size didn't matter much in swimming. He practiced and became a very good swimmer. In junior high he passed his life-saving test and joined the school swim team. Because schools were **segregated**, African American children were not allowed to swim in the city swim meets. But they did compete among themselves. They knew they were faster in some events than the city champions were.

The Bolden home in Columbia, South Carolina

Charles became a champion swimmer. He spent his summers as a lifeguard at the local swimming pool. Being a good swimmer paid off in a big way one summer. Charles's cousin Eugene was visiting from New York. Charles and Eugene decided to go down to the Columbia River dam. Eugene could not swim. He fell off the dam and disappeared under the cold water. While Charles's frightened buddies looked on helplessly, Charles bravely jumped into the dark, swirling water and rescued his terrified cousin.

Charles (in the chair, at left) sits with a baby cousin in 1954.

Charles attended C. A. Johnson High School,
where his father coached football.

Charles became a hero. Eugene would never forget his visit to Columbia. But Coach Bolden was a no-nonsense dad. He gave Charles and Eugene a good scolding for being on the river dam in the first place!

Charles attended C. A. Johnson High School. By this time his dad was the football coach there. Coach Bolden was loved and respected. The school stadium was later named after him.

More than anything, Charles, Jr., wanted his father to be proud of him. He tried hard to become one of the starting players on the football team. His friend Dickie later recalled, "Little Charles was a pretty good player, but he didn't weigh enough. Coach Bolden wasn't about to take the chance of him being clobbered by a visiting team. And so Little Charles sat on the sidelines at the big games and helped call the plays."

One day Charles finally got his wish to be a football hero. During a 1963 state championship game, his team's quarterback was hurt. Charles took over and helped his team win.

Charles 3 years later

Charles's 1960 school photo

Chapter 5

Ready to Go!

Charles worked very hard in high school. His high grades made him a member of the National Honor Society. He served as editor of the school newspaper and president of the student council. He was also a member of the chorus and the athletic club. He **persevered** in his studies and graduated second in his class in 1964.

Still, Charles had to **overcome** obstacles when he tried to get into college. The University of South Carolina turned him down. No African American had ever attended that university. Charles's mother and father found out about schools outside of South Carolina. Going away to college would cost more, but his parents were **determined** that he should go. Charles wanted to go to college more than anything.

After reading about the United States Naval Academy, Charles said to his dad, "I really want to join the Marine Corps. The Academy is where I should go." But his father knew that Charles would need a sponsor from South Carolina to write a letter supporting Charles. At that time African Americans had a hard time finding support.

Charles tried anyway. He wrote to South Carolina's members of Congress. He even wrote to the Vice President of the United States, Lyndon Johnson. He received a letter of support from Vice President Johnson. But Charles had to have the support of someone in Congress. In spite of Charles's **efforts**, no one from South Carolina wrote a letter.

Charles had his heart set on going to the Naval Academy.

Charles was disappointed. But he did not give up. He knew that somehow there had to be a way. He continued to write to anyone who might help. He was determined to overcome this challenge. When Vice President Lyndon Johnson became President of the United States in 1963, Charles wrote to him again.

Charles's **persistence** paid off. In 1964 he heard that William L. Dawson, an African American congressman from Chicago, had agreed to sponsor him for the Naval Academy. After many letters and much hard work, Charles entered the Naval Academy in 1964.

First day at the Naval Academy.

Charles at the Academy in 1964

Like all students at the Naval Academy, Charles found the classes difficult. He had to learn different languages, study math and different sciences, and still go through very tough military training.

Charles and his dad at the Academy

At that time few African Americans had studied at the Naval Academy. It was hard being one of the few African Americans among thousands of students at the Academy. But Charles was ready for the challenge. He made friends with his classmates, and he impressed his teachers with his positive attitude and intelligence. Charles became the first African American class president in the history of the Naval Academy. He graduated from the Academy in 1968.

Charles and his mother outside the Academy in 1964

When Charles graduated from the Naval Academy in 1968, he married his high-school sweetheart, Alexis "Jackie" Walker of Columbia. Their son, Anthony Ché, was born on June 9, 1971. Their daughter, Kelly, was born on March 17, 1976.

The next step in Charles's plan was to join the Marine Corps. Only a small number of Naval Academy graduates could move on to the Marine

Charles joined the Marine Corps in 1968.

Corps, but Charles was selected. He went through the difficult six-month training period, where he learned the basic skills of being a soldier. He graduated second in his basic-training class. Charles then decided he wanted to become a Marine pilot.

Charles's wife, Jackie Walker

For the next two years, Charles learned how to fly planes. He trained in Florida, Mississippi, and Texas. Soon he was fighting in the Vietnam War. He piloted more than 100 flights during the war. Sometimes Charles and his crew flew at night. Sometimes they flew in bad weather. During the entire year that Charles served in the Vietnam War, he was always able to guide his plane safely back to the base.

During that time Charles was training to become a test pilot for the Navy. In 1979 he made an important decision. He decided to apply to become an astronaut. In 1980 he was chosen as an astronaut **candidate**. There were 78 astronauts at that time. Only 4 were African Americans.

Charles's astronaut training lasted a year. He learned how to make emergency repairs. He learned how to walk in space. He learned how to fly a space shuttle. Then he waited for 5 years. Finally, in 1986 Charles flew on his first flight into space as the pilot of the space shuttle *Columbia*.

Charles with his wife and children today

Chapter 6

A Modern-Day Hero

Charles made 3 trips into space after his flight on the *Columbia*. During his career as an astronaut, he spent almost 700 hours in outer space. In 1992 he became Assistant Deputy Administrator at the NASA Headquarters in Washington, D.C. Later he became a major general in the U.S. Marines and Deputy Commander of the United States forces in Japan.

General Bolden has traveled around the United States to visit schools and talk to students. He reminds them of how important it is to stay in school. "Mainly," he says, "have a dream. Don't sell yourself short. Believe you can do it, and you will."

Ethel Bolden, Charles's mother, still lives in the home where Charles grew up. She is proud of her son. She says that Charles was not a genius in the usual meaning of the word. He faced many challenges on the road to becoming an astronaut. He had to study and work hard to make good grades in school. "The genius is in knowing how hard it is and doing it anyway," she says.

Charles served as pilot of the *Discovery* in 1990

General Bolden has received many honors and awards for his hard work and special abilities. One very special award was an

Warren and Charles with their mother in 1994

honorary Doctor of Science Degree from the University of South Carolina in 1984. This is the same college that turned him away 20 years earlier.

Another award came on February 13, 1999, when General Bolden was made a member of the South Carolina Hall of Fame.

Charles with his mother in 1999

General Bolden said of his first space voyage, "It was more than I had even dreamed of—a fantastic, **uplifting** experience. I can't explain all the feelings, but I know for sure there's something out there other than space." And after 4 voyages into space, he still feels that way.

The city of Columbia, South Carolina, and the rest of the United States are very proud of their native son, who overcame many challenges in order to make his dreams come true. To people everywhere, he says, "You can, too!"

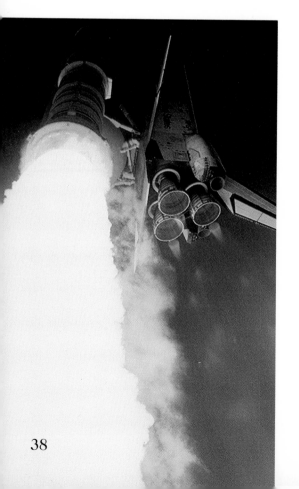

Glossary

candidate someone who wants and prepares for a job

challenge a difficulty

determined having one's mind made up; certain

effort the act of trying

frustrating disappointing

gauge an instrument that measures

gravity the pull of the earth

launch the send-off into space

Mission Control a center on the ground where trained people watch over and help guide space shuttles and other space vessels

obstacle something that stands in the way

overcome to achieve in spite of troubles and roadblocks

persevere to keep trying

persistence the act of never giving up

regulator a device for controlling the flow of gases or liquids

segregated separated; set apart

uplifting making something better

Index